/1995

DATE			

Nights of the Pufflings

written and photo-illustrated by Bruce McMillan

Houghton Mifflin Company
Boston 1995

Fyrir íslenska vin minn
Kristján Egilsson

Iceland

These photos of North Atlantic puffins and young pufflings (Fratercula arctica arctica) were taken during the spring and summer of 1993 on the island of Heimaey *(HAY • mah • ay),* Iceland. The island is located six miles (10 km) off Iceland's southwest coast. Heimaey, only five square miles (13.4 km²) in size, is the largest of the Westmann Islands. It has about 5,000 residents and an economy based on fishing. The oldest part of the island is merely 12,000 years old, formed from a volcanic eruption. The newest part came into existence in the winter of 1973, when a new eruption increased the size of the island by one-fifth. Ironically, the still-steaming lava that borders the east side of town lies within view of a glacier (seen in the facing photo) on the main island of Iceland.

The photographs were made using a Nikon F4/MF23 with 24, 50, 105 micro, 180, 300, and 600 mm lenses. When possible, the camera was mounted on a tripod. Many of the photos were taken from inside a camouflage tent-blind. A polarizing filter was sometimes used during the day, or a blue color filter at night. Lighting at night was a mix of two flash units, car headlights, flashlights, and/or street lamps. The film was Kodachrome 64 Professional (for both day and night photos) and Kodachrome 200 Professional (for certain night photos only), all processed by Kodalux.

This book was made possible through the help and assistance of:
Einar Gustavsson, the Iceland Tourist Board;
Kristján Egilsson, Director, The Museum of Natural History and Aquarium in Vestmannaeyjar;
Óskar Sigurðsson, Stóhöfði lighthouse keeper and puffin naturalist;
Rafn Pálsson, Manager, Hótel Brædraborg; Páll Pálsson, Captain, PH *Viking*;
Halla Ósk Ólafsdóttir, Arnar Ingi Ingimarsson,
Arndis Bára Ingimarsdóttir, and Maria Sif Ingimarsdóttir, the children;
Ólafur Ólafsson and Ingimar Georgsson, the children's fathers;
and Brett McMillan, photo assistant.

Designed by Bruce McMillan

Library of Congress Cataloging-in-Publication Data

McMillan, Bruce.
  Nights of the pufflings / written and photo-illustrated by Bruce McMillan.
      p.   cm.   ISBN 0-395-70810-9
      1. Puffins—Iceland—Juvenile literature.   [1. Puffins.
  2. Zoology—Iceland.]   I. Title.
  QL696.C42M39   1995   94-14808
  598.3'3—dc20   CIP
                          AC

Printed in Singapore   TWP   10   9   8   7   6   5   4   3   2   1

Heimaey Island *(HAY • mah • ay)*, Iceland
April

Halla *(HATTL • lah)* searches the sky every day. As she watches from high on a cliff overlooking the sea, she spots her first puffin of the season. She whispers to herself, "Lundi" *(LOON • dah),* which means "puffin" in Icelandic.

Soon the sky is speckled with them—puffins, puffins
everywhere. Millions of these birds are returning from their winter
at sea. They are coming back to Halla's island and the nearby
uninhabited islands to lay eggs and raise puffin chicks. It's the
only time they come ashore.

While Halla and her friends are at school in the village beneath the cliffs, the puffins continue to land. These "clowns of the sea" return to the same burrows year after year. Once back, they busy themselves getting their underground nests ready. Halla and all the children of Heimaey *(HAY • mah • ay)* can only wait and dream of the nights of the pufflings yet to come.

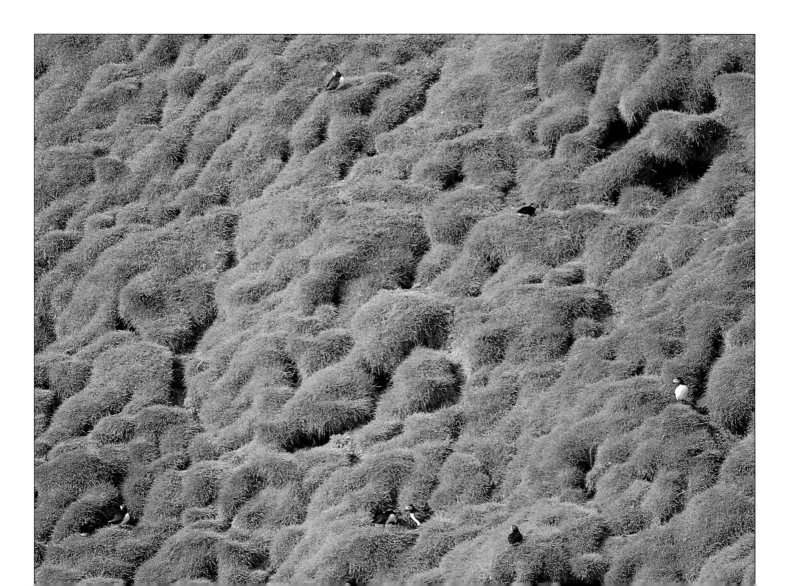

On the weekends, Halla and her friends climb over the cliffs to watch the birds. They see puffin pairs *tap-tap-tap* their beaks together. Each pair they see will soon tend an egg. Deep inside the cliffs that egg will hatch a chick. That chick will grow into a young puffling. That puffling will take its first flight. The nights of the pufflings will come.

In the summer, while Halla splashes in the cold ocean water, the puffins also splash. The sea below the cliffs is dotted with puffins bobbing on the waves. Like Halla, many puffins that ride the waves close to shore are young. The older birds usually fly further out to sea where the fishing is better. The grown-up puffins have to catch lots of fish, because now that it's summer they are feeding more than just themselves.

Halla's friend, Arnar Ingi *(ATT • nar ING • ee),* spies a puffin
overhead. "Fisk" *(FIHSK),* he whispers as he gazes at the
returning puffin's bill full of fish. The puffin eggs have hatched,
and the parents are bringing home fish to feed their chicks. The
nights of the pufflings are still long weeks away, but Arnar Ingi
thinks about getting some cardboard boxes ready.

Halla and her friends never see the chicks—only the chicks' parents see them. The baby puffins never come out. They stay safely hidden in the long dark tunnels of their burrows. But Halla and her friends hear them calling out for food. *"Peep-peep-peep."* The growing chicks are hungry. Their parents have to feed them—sometimes ten times a day—and carry many fish in their bills.

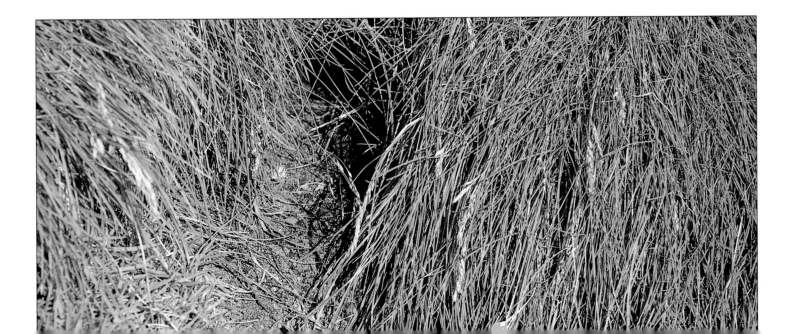

All summer long the adult puffins fish and tend to their feathers. By August, flowering baldusbrá *(BAL • durs • broh)* blanket the burrows. With the baldusbrá in full bloom, Halla knows that the wait is over. The hidden chicks have grown into young pufflings. The pufflings are ready to fly and will at last venture out into the night. Now it's time.

It's time for Halla and her friends to get out their boxes and flashlights for the nights of the pufflings. Starting tonight, and for the next two weeks, the pufflings will be leaving for their winter at sea. Halla and her friends will spend each night searching for stranded pufflings that don't make it to the water. But the village cats and dogs will be searching, too. It will be a race to see who finds the stray pufflings first. By ten o'clock the streets of Heimaey are alive with roaming children.

In the darkness of night, the pufflings leave their burrows for their first flight. It's a short, wing-flapping trip from the high cliffs. Most of the birds splash-land safely in the sea below. But some get confused by the village lights—perhaps they think the lights are moonbeams reflecting on the water. Hundreds of the pufflings crash-land in the village every night. Unable to take off from flat ground, they run around and try to hide. Dangers await. Even if the cats and dogs don't get them, the pufflings might get run over by cars or trucks.

Halla and her friends race to the rescue. Armed with their flashlights, they wander through the village. They search dark places. Halla yells out "puffling" in Icelandic. "Lundi pysja!" *(LOON•dah PEESH•yar).* She has spotted one. When the puffling runs down the street, she races after it, grabs it, and nestles it in her arms. Arnar Ingi catches one, too. No sooner are the pufflings safe in the cardboard boxes than more of them land nearby. "Lundi pysja! Lundi pysja!"

For two weeks all the children of Heimaey sleep late in the day so they can stay out at night. They rescue thousands of pufflings. There are pufflings, pufflings everywhere, and helping hands too —even though the pufflings instinctively nip at helping fingers. Every night Halla and her friends take the rescued pufflings home. The next day they send their guests on their way. Halla meets her friends and, with the boxes full of pufflings, they hike down to the beach.

27

It's time to set the pufflings free. Halla releases one first. She holds it up so that it will get used to flapping its wings. Then, with the puffling held snugly in her hands, she counts "Einn–tveir–ÞRÍR!" *(EYN–TVAIR–THEER)* as she swings the puffling three times between her legs. The last swing is the highest, launching the bird up in the air and out over the water beyond the surf. It's only the second time this puffling has flown, so it flutters just a short distance before safely splash-landing.

Day after day Halla's pufflings paddle away, until the nights of the pufflings are over for the year. As she watches the last of the pufflings and adult puffins leave for their winter at sea, Halla bids them farewell until next spring. She wishes them a safe journey as she calls out "goodbye, goodbye" in Icelandic. "Bless, bless!"

Puffins and Pufflings

When pufflings leave Heimaey, they quickly learn to fish for themselves. In only eight weeks, many fly more than a thousand miles (1,600 km) to the waters off Newfoundland. They mature a year or two before returning to Heimaey. At about five years old they begin pairing and mating. Each pair raises a chick every year. Once the chick becomes a puffling and leaves its burrow, the young bird is on its own, and can live as long as 29 years.

North Atlantic puffins are easy to identify in the sky by their rapid wing beats of 300–400 per minute. They fly as fast as 50 mph (80 km/h). Underwater, puffins "fly" during 20- to 30-second dives and catch small fish such as sand lance and capelin. Using their tongues to hold the fish in their bills, they usually carry from 4 to 20. The record is 64 tiny fish!

Puffins are sometimes called "clowns of the sea" because of their bright bills and awkward antics. They are clumsy fliers during takeoffs and landings because they have chunky bodies and short wings. On a calm day they have difficulty taking off from a level surface such as the ocean, and it looks like they're running on the water. Their landings are no more graceful, as they often crash-land, tumble, and collide.

At sea in winter, puffin beaks are smaller in size and without bright colors. Their faces are dusky gray. At the end of winter, and while still at sea, puffins shed their feathers and grow new ones—they molt. They aren't able to fly until replacement feathers grow in. In spring the puffins arrive at their burrows with new feathers, bright orange-red legs and feet, and bills trimmed in yellow. Their feathered faces are sparkling white, dotted with eyes circled in red. In this newly-colored breeding plumage they have sometimes been called "sea parrots."

North Atlantic puffins *(Fratercula arctica)* live in the ocean from Maine to Canada to Greenland to Iceland to Norway to Ireland to Great Britain. They are commonly called puffins in the United States, Canada, and Great Britain, quilángaq in Greenland, lundi in Iceland, and lunde in Norway and Denmark. Two other kinds of puffins, horned puffins *(Fratercula corniculata)* with yellow and orange bills, and tufted puffins *(Lunda cirrhata)* with orange-red bills, all black lower bodies, and long yellow plumes on their heads, live in the North Pacific.

Bibliography

Dennis, Roy. *Puffins*. Lanark, Scotland: Colin Baxter Photography, Ltd., 1990.

Einarsson, Þorsteinn. Reykjavík, Iceland: *Guide to the Birds of Iceland*. Örn Og Örlygur Publishing House, 1991.

Harris, M.P. *The Puffin*. Calton, England: T & A D Poyser, Ltd., 1984.

Lockley, R.M. *Puffins*. New York: The Devin-Adair Company, 1953.

Martin, Lynne. *Puffin, Bird of the Open Seas*. New York: William Morrow and Company, 1976.

Nettelship, David N. and Birkhead, Tim R., ed. *The Atlantic Alcidae*. San Diego: Academic Press, 1985.